FOR BLUE
Butterflies

JESSICA L. IRIZARRY
POETIC JUSTICE

Miles
"Carrot Top"

Remember do all things
with love
- Poetic Justice

Jessica L. Irizarry
(Poetic Justice)
For Blue Butterflies

Perth Amboy, NJ

Book Layout:
Jen Henderson at Wild Words Formatting

Front Cover and Book Layout Design:
Rebecacovers-Fivver

Photography:
Photos_by_Nichole.Marie

Printed in the USA
For Blue Butterflies/ Jessica Irizarry-1st Ed.
ISBN: 978-0-578-61394-9
Library of Congress Control Number: 2021915410

Connect with author:
Instagram: Justicep0etry
Email: PoeticallyJess714@gmail.com

Dedicated to my beautiful daughters *Amaia* and *Jaelani*, I am proud to be your mommy. I have prayed for the blessing of your existence all my life; you both are my 'why'. The gift of your life has led me to be a better version of myself. Let this book be living proof that dreams do come true with hard work, focus, and dedication. May life always teach you to make beautiful memories through art and with art, whatever your art may be. This book is mommy's journey through life, growth, love, forgiveness, loss, and change, so far. I love you! Remember, I have your back and we will always have each other when you face any challenges this world brings before you. Everything I will ever do in this life will always be for you.

To my nephews, *Josiah,* and *Giovani.* Watching you grow has been an honor. Thank you for being the joy and push I have needed early in my life to come this far. I will always lead you boys by example, and this is just the first of many. You are the reminder in my life that happiness is just one joke away. I hope this book inspires you to follow your dreams, give love selflessly, and find peace where pain exists. Titi loves you always.

To *Lyric* and *Eros*, you both have won my heart repeatedly. You will always be the extended family in my life, the children I learned to love because you loved me in return. In a short amount of time, you have taught me some unbelievably valuable lessons in life as a parent and as a friend. I am grateful God has brought us together. I am proud of the young individuals you have grown to be. Continue to strive for your absolute best. I know you are both destined for greatness in this world. Love you endlessly, M.J.

A MESSAGE FROM THE AUTHOR

It is almost unrealistic to extend gratitude and thank you to the many influences I have been blessed with throughout life, but here I will do my absolute best to honor those for leaving their true mark in my journey as a growing writer and poet. Taking this project on has been such a wonderful trip for me. I owe my courage and faith to God above everything. It is also important to highlight the many days I spent with writer's block and unwavering inspiration. As an aspiring author we want to produce the absolute best product. We want the closest product we can create to perfection. After almost a 2-year process, 'For Blue Butterflies' has come to fruition. The title of this book was inspired shortly after my father's passing. I would take long walks and runs, during those times and write my ideas down or complete an entire poem before I completed my walk or run. In all those moments, I was always followed by a butterfly. Whether it be on the track or a soccer field or a butterfly conservatory. I genuinely believe it was a sign to follow my dream of always becoming a published author, thus here we are.

Before I decided to write 'For Blue Butterflies' I needed to open my heart to what my true calling was to understand how to justly water my roots and be able to share them with the world. It required me to break myself down and reconstruct myself at the core. All this to give myself the best chance I had to tap into something deeper than what we face on the surface daily.

This book is my 'baby'. It was constructed from the depths of my soul's closet to the very shelves I have long aspired to be part of. From young love and lust to grief, pain, loss and renovation, my final product brings me full circle. The title itself and every chapter begins with the letter 'F', to coincide with 'father', whom I made a point of honoring in my very first project as a writer; because his demise opened my eyes to the very meaning of, tomorrow is not promised. I pray that in all those low moments, my fellow readers can create something beautiful out of it. *For Blue Butterflies'* truly captures my highs, lows, and true colors of all that makes me who I am/was, the product of my own environment.

If we do anything right in life let it be leading everyday with true joy and producing love in all that we give to one another. As a friendly reminder: When a poet falls in love with you, you will live on forever.

Sincerely,

Jessica L. Irizarry
Poetic Justice

Acknowledgments

Thank you to my mentor, best friend and role model, *Janine*. Your endless help and dedication to my success comes second to none. Thank you for taking on the many phone calls, text messages, voice clips at all hours of the day, and my endless questions. For taking time out of your busy days to guide me, reassure me, critique me, assist me, and listen to me. You have supported my craft and have always pushed me to elevate regardless of my procrastination. Thank you for paving the way for me Janine. I could not have done any of this without your guidance, honesty, and exposure. You are a light and because of you I shine too.

To my mother, *Nilsa*, thank you for always pushing me to follow my dreams. May this book make you prouder of me. I am grateful to have had you around long enough to share this milestone with you. Thank you for paying attention, for supporting me without obvious behavior and for surprising me with your devotion to detail when I least expected it. I love you.

To my accountability partner, *Chloe*, thank you for our writing sessions. The numerous days and nights you forced me to stand up on the spot, perform and perfect my poetry, my stage presence, and my delivery. You have truly shaped who I am as a poet and performer. Thank you for always believing in me. For showing up when no one else would and for always pushing me way out of my comfort zone. As children to our adulthood, you have always given me reason to feel inspired. You brought out of me what I was always afraid to expose. You allowed me to flourish without changing who I was at my core. I am ever grateful for you.

To my uncle **Timothy**, it is because of you I explored poetry and writing at such a young age. As a child you would sit me down and share your poetry with me. You would tell me expressing your love through poetry was true romance. Thank you for planting the seed, look what it has grown into.

To my support system:

Juan, you have saved my life in ways many would not understand. Thank you for being the big brother I always prayed for. For teaching me 'zen' and connecting with me on spiritual levels only God could have orchestrated so beautifully.

Jeana, to say thank you would not be enough. Your honesty and positive energy have always been on time. Thank you for our meditation sessions when I experienced the lowest levels of inspiration and the darkest of emotions in times of grief. Thank you for always coming to support my performances, for promoting my videos/recordings and being such a huge fan of my work.

Jessica, the doctor, my big sister, and above all an angel sent. Thank you for grounding me when it seemed almost impossible for me. Thank you for reminding me to always be intentional with all that I do in my journey through life and for sharing with me your true sentiments of my poetry, pushing me to be my best.

Jorge, my partner in blue, thank you for encouraging me every chance you got while we worked the streets together. Your days of listening and helping me put out my message through poetry will always be appreciated. Thank you for pushing me and praying for my success. Your motivational speeches and tough love to get this work out has always reminded me there are people who needed me to be their voice.

Nichole/Talez Photography, a growing business destined for all this world has to offer. I am ever grateful for your geniuses, creativity, and you taking time to capture a photo that speaks volumes for my story. Thank you for helping me recreate what lies deep within my heart with the proper focus of your camera lenses. I am grateful for your support and consistent friendship. Thank you for your listening ears and warm shoulders in those times I felt lost. Thank you for reminding me to write it out first.

Christine, after many years of feeling uninspired and stuck you awakened the poet in me. For that and much more I will forever be grateful for you. Thank you for allowing me the platform to share with you my work and providing me the criticism I needed to push myself to greater heights. Thank you for providing me the space needed to focus and create, I deeply appreciate you. Cheers to our foundation, poetry! Because of you my appetite for writing remains passionately active. You have given me some of the greatest memories in writing. From our first date to our first performance together, I could not have shared those special moments with anyone else. Thank you for listening and reading when I was unsure of the flow of my work. You inspire me to be fearless. I cannot wait for you to release your work so the world can see what I have always seen in you, your amazing, unmatched talent. I Love You without boundary, Bee.

Lastly, to all my unnamed fans and supporters, I am grateful for all of you. I pray I can always deliver words that resonate with you. Each one of you adds a different taste to my writer's world. You have inspired me in ways I find difficult to articulate at times. Some words may not be enough to express my true sentiments, however, my gratitude, love, and appreciation pours into my poetry. I pray I fuel your soul with a light made strictly for you and as the universe intended. Thank you for being a guiding force in my journey of authorship. Remember, do all things with love and be unafraid to find your voice.

Remembering the Life of My Father

My father, Ruben 'Giro' Irizarry-Cedeno is no longer here to be part of this accomplishment, but I would like to shed light on his life and the impact and influence he had in completing 'For Blue Butterflies'. While it pains me to revisit this grief, I love my father and I know he loved me too. As proud as he always told me he was, I wish he could be present to share this book with me. His demise opened a new portal of my poetic craft, and it has also locked me out, placing me in a dark writer's block. However, the chapter dedicated to my father, 'Funeral', brought some beautifully crafted poetry that could not have taken place if not for my healing, understanding, and forgiving process of his life and death.

Being the youngest of his siblings, my father required extra nurturing, guidance, and attention. That of which he suffered no lack thereof. He struggled a great deal at a young age, which translated into the poor habits he had as an adult. I wish during his lowest moments I had a better understanding of his story however, I can now speak confidently about who I believe my dad was. My father was a selfless and selfish man all in one. He lied often to benefit himself. He was the Puerto Rican version of 'the boy who cried wolf', always needed help, but always offered his help. He died owing many people money and answers, but of those people my brother and I were the ones who needed it most. Ruben was a handsome oxymoron to say the least.

My father's image is sacred to me regardless of his short comings in his and mine. Thus, I want you to remember him via my perspective and not through those foul stories' others would share about him. I want to remember him as the man who would secretly save me when I was in a rut. I want to remember him as the man who would call me every day striving to improve on our father-daughter relationship. Remember him for the man who would hug me ever so tightly, enough to exhaust the air in my lungs, each time he saw me. I want to remember him for the man who cried, as he silently wanted my forgiveness for his absence in my childhood. The man who would pinch my cheeks giggling saying 'ju daddy loves you' in his heavy Spanish accent. Recall him for the man who would always wear a #2 pencil between his ear and silk hair. He was an artist in every sense of the word and a jokester. I remember him as the man who would visit my elementary school and hang on the fence watching me play as he would call out my name, ever so happy to see me. I remember him as the man who loved his time in the kitchen. A man who loved his kids, grandkids, nieces, and nephews.

Daddy, I miss you a great deal. Thank you for being my guardian angel. Thank you for giving me that last bit of motivation to fulfill one of my lifelong dreams. Wait for me, I have a long journey ahead of me. I Love You.

TABLE OF CONTENTS

Chapter 1

FREEDOM

INSIGHT

Writer's block is a very real feeling. The 'Freedom' chapter is what broke the ice for me after not wanting to write again. I spent approximately 3 years avoiding my talent. I stood in my own way knowing I had something beautiful to share with the world. I knew I had things I may have left unsaid that needed to come to light. In this chapter you get my breakthrough moment. I made the decision to stand for myself, something I stopped doing whenever I allowed life to knock me down. It is said in the late hours an artist creates their best work. Those words have never rung truer. I wrote these poems at approximately 4a.m. and it was during this time I realized, I am a poet & a writer, I should never let my calling go unanswered. The point of all this is, do not stand in your way. You have layers, let them be peeled back so others can learn your true self.

FREEDOM

I am a victim of internal damage, full of metaphorical phases that revert to anything and everything that is symbolic of you.

Delicate like a glass bottle; I have shattered at the reminiscent troubles stained in my memory. There, here, and everywhere lies a moment to reflect.

In my mirror you exist, still and staring back at me, I am broken.

I piece together what is left of me and begin a new journey where music follows me, where your footprints pave the way, and in the clouds are silhouette paintings of storms that slowly come to an end, bringing gardens full of heaven, a fresh breeze that uplifts the ugly facets we made and then, the crash of my emotions wreak havoc.

Once again, I find my mind floating in an open pool of tears.

My thoughts have been drowned out.

My doubts have caused a plague and all that was once clarity is now the totality of vague. Attacked by fear, controlled by the unknown and I have burdened my heart; thus, without you I flat line.

My stability is laid over our foundation; I waited for you, my greatest of patience.

Without reversing any damage, I find you at the end of this exploration as if you were my guiding light.

I am a message in a bottle, left at sea, traveling with each wave, hoping to be caught.

I am guilty of one thing. It is my cry, my pleading, my need for you indeed.

It has been a long time, but never the right time.

Today, however I reconnect my pain with the next line.

Your like glue stuck on my every rhyme.

I search for healing that of which I cannot find.

I search for answers that of which you won't supply.

I search for you, but you run and hide.

I find peace on the outside, with unsettled gut-wrenching sadness I drive myself crazy thinking of you.

It's a mystical madness that collapses over me each time I relive the life we once lived.

A prayer for you, my ever after, this is true.

A revelation of truth, I stand before you in my nude.

I unveil my most kept secrets and you free me like doves, we meet again.

Never to repeat this absence.

A poet is free of all that defines writer's block.

CREATIVE STATEMENT (FOR THE ARTIST IN SHE)

To be able to replace the wanting in your soul while facing the hypocrisies of the crisis of our life, we...are trapped and mind controlled to be unified with what the eyes of the universe has classified and specified for us.

You, you are not supposed to be you!

You are supposed to be like them!

Because they perceive what their eyes do not see...only the deep can comprehend what this even means.

Like shadow puppets, like ghost that need your company they are on you like white on rice.

Watching and reviewing whose, what is, when is, where's and how's...life...your wrong doings...'ya' doings and who you are screwing?

So, you sink into the depths of what creativity can measure.

Only to submit to your self-preservation for the sake of satisfying the ego, super ego, id...that immediate kind of pleasure.

In turn you rebel the ugliness of ignorance, the opinion of the uneducated and inexperienced.

They shout their double standards at you not quite understanding the standards that separate you from the understandings they stand under because they are nobody's! They are beneath you.

Like the grounds they worship but the ones you step on.

The likings of their kind but get no social media likes.

Trend setters but aren't even trending.

Gold diggers with no treasures, lack of leadership so they follow and you... stay behind.

Your creativity resets the twilight zone trapped within your mind.

Unwind the capacities of life.

The "us" kind move like chess pieces, at the right time.

In tune with your intuition.

Closed doors leave room for the pondering, how do you do it?

Well, we retract your statements and rebirth them through art.

That's what sets us apart.

Possessed by our fierce like leadership, the wanting of our souls does not need replacements.

Rather blatant statements of the glorifications of our greatness.

So please, do not question my authority to rule my life because I'm sure you have no answers to how you live your 'trife'.

Do not tell me how to sip juice from my sippy cup because I am sure you use a straw, that's talented behavior for... you suck!

And the next time you feel the urge to disturb my peace of mind and make my business your expertise and you a testimonial witness of me, check yourself before you...before you... wreck yourself!

Reflection

This mirror reflection whispers to me you are more human than hero.

More than a band aid drenched in lonely.

If only I could be satisfied with this empty matrimony.

I have nothing but me.

I've been chasing glass homes filled with regret.

Factors of the old me still exist, that not caring has become a normal habit of satisfactory.

Yet somehow, I manage to smile.

If only I could see through the looking glass.

Find the blueprints of the intimate details that make me a whole me.

If only I could understand that life is like seashells.

One washed up on the shore and another sails right on through.

The water comes striking just to take back what it left you.

If only I understood why I could never find balance to this life scale.

Perhaps I'm a black cloud or the journey right now is too strong for me to fight.

Perhaps I was made to seek strays, made to derail, made to crumble only to build me up again.

Oh, sweet architect carefully layout my pieces for me.

Like tsunami emotions drown out my tearless cries, I see you with these blind eyes.

I see how timid your reach for love is. How fear is your shadow. How change is your enemy.

How no matter what angle you take to refocus your views there is always a slight misread in the multitude of perceptions of...you. Who are you?

What is your purpose? Why have you found a comfort in complacency when you have been taught that it will only kill you?

You are more peace than you are war.

Yet somehow, you are trapped in this web of deceit and constant struggle.

Without it, there is no progress.

You are more major than you are minor.

Your reflection is few in between those black & white keys that unlock hidden doors.

If only I was a vampire so my reflection would just disappear, and I no longer had to look at flaws that blankly stare back at me.

Beneath my surface is where you find things that have been buried and never forgotten.

You are more beautiful than you are disaster.

If only I could discover a mystical pot of treasure at the end of every rainbow, that we all know does not exist but secretly wish it did.

If only people understood the power in words, the power of silence, and the damage in actions.

I unfold the gravity words hold to center myself because who I see has become more priceless than gold.

If only I knew my self-worth and healed sooner from self-hurt.

If only I could stop searching for my reflection and let it seek me, like freedom overcoming slavery.

Escaping! Renewing! Reinventing!

I wish I could die, resurrect, and come back as someone spiteful enough to hate you.

VERBAL PORTRAIT

I have written enough poetry to reincarnate the colors of your soul and resurface undamaged textures of your flesh.

Burdened by wordless verses I find courage in painting your portrait without the vision or purpose.

We hide behind scriptures designed to teach us our service without understanding the promise of our fortress.

Continuously reading signs of misfortune, a Mona Lisa distorted, and foreign hearted lovers aborted.

Illusion like Picasso pigments stained in my memory like the weeping woman.

I, I am not a painter, but the artist in me is inspired to save her as if removing all darkness and splattering color everywhere is the solution.

This journal is heart surgery.

I continue filling spaces in these pages praying God answer me with his saving graces.

I let the bible take me to forbidden places.

Bite the apple of Eden but do not mistake me for a heathen.

I am a rose that grew from concrete withstanding the changes of season.

Loves taken the back seat, but if you let me, I will keep writing to the tunes of R&B or let Mozart fine tune the melodies in these black and white keys so I can get lost in the realm of what use to be.

Reminisce like you are a throwback on repeat.

If you let me, I can be the Jack to your Rose, and paint you like one of those French girls.

There is no room for error.

I created a picture vivid enough to cure blindness, but what if pain was heredity and it was designed to guide us?

Time cannot be borrowed

I try seeing life without you, but we do not get to die without making things right.

Attention is expensive to pay.

Your smile paints the background of my world.

Let us stay forever young.

Love forever elementary.

Paint freely of thoughts unspoken, speak freely of words unheard of.

You release endorphins in me.

I experience levitations even stoners would not believe, but if I cannot stay high off you, the idea I just could not conceive.

Let us exchange energy like cosmic proportions because without you is living without poetry. Perhaps that is why I covered the walls of my home with you, art in every aspect of anew.

Chapter 2

FROM WILLIAMSBURG

INSIGHT

From Williamsburg is not about the city itself, but about a person. This chapter puts the reader on a journey of different moments shared together and apart with my childhood love. Through lust, love, and destruction, these pieces reveal what a teenage love was like from my perspective. I learned how others at that time loved and lusted over people, including themselves.

714

It has been 14 years since I last felt her early morning presence.

14 years when I last smelled the sweet scent of Dior as she misted her inner wrists and flipped her hair.

It has been 14 years of an uphill battle, 14 years of joys and despair.

14 years of trials and tribulations and 14yrs later we are still here.

It has been 14 years, that's 5,110 days, but who is counting?

It was a scent all too familiar that only existed on her smooth, caramel skin.

14 years since I last tasted her from within as she seeped through my pores reeking of addict, Dior.

As a child who was I to even comprehend this intense appetite for a person who knew nothing of satisfying cravings, because after all, we were just two hounds searching and preying, hunting for our next fix.

Her masochistic ways played with my psyche for 14 years.

A natural erotica full of disasters because I couldn't understand why for 14 years, I allowed her to inhibit me from shutting down a 6th sense only she could trigger.

It has been 14 years since I last smelled her sweet scent of Dior.

Addicted to the chase for 14 years and more.

It has been 14 years of her embed memories lingering in the air I inhale, but 14 years later she no longer flows in the wind of sweet, misted Dior trapped within four walls we slept in, but never existed together in.

14 years since the early mornings of you strategically pairing your garments to feel your finest self before work.

14 years since I last watched her mist her inner wrists, kiss my cheek ever so gently leaving me with nothing more than her perfume.

Poetry While You Sleep

I wanna' write poetry that changes the alignment of stars in all that makes our galaxy.

Make poetic history with words that have never been heard before.

Then watch you as you doze off into the night while I read to you.

Praying you see the beauty in falling and me catching you while you dream.

I send you off with words you've inspired.

If I said I didn't enjoy this, then the devil is a liar.

The tranquil of your faint breathing brings healing to my scars.

I can spend hours watching you and even longer holding you hoping you can feel the nervous beats in my heart.

There's a tremor in my hands as I connect pencil with paper.

I inhale some of you mixed with some vapor. My truth is self-tailored.

I am your voice, you are my lyric; you are my action, I am your silence.

I wanna' write pieces so you never die; compose written arts so our love never subsides.

You are my natural habitat. Let us procreate poetic infants that take over the world.

Help me distinguish between reality and existence.

I read so you are at peace, I write so you understand my ease and I perform like I wanna' relive this moment so the world puts our record on repeat.

I expose myself to you, to think and to feel.

It's an emotion that creates a vulnerable chemistry we cannot resist.

As you sleep, I want to decipher your meditations, strike chords in your crevasses wondering if you can feel my energy piercing through your rapid eye movement.

I wonder if you will allow me to write pieces, so the world knows of my muse.

Steadfastly bridging the gap between where we stand now to the whisper of your 'I DO'.

Publish books that tell a never lived anecdote endlessly loving you through an infinite number of definitions made just for us.

Poetry is my poison, and you are my antidote. I wanna' write poetry that cures your broken heart, poetry that seals with a kiss, and some poetry that brings happiness to the scared little girl you desperately try to outgrow.

Make poems that sing like music. Sing like sounds of love and life, giving meaning to us at the end of our night.

I wanna' write so you can reconnect with me and remember our first time.

Make smooth and deep poetry, like sex, I wanna' write but take my time, making sure not to miss any stroke of genius or confuse the next line with a poor rhyme.

It intensifies as I continue to pour myself into you.

At night I wonder if you crave me at your side.

A girl can dream right?

Thus, I use poetry to reveal my true lies.

BONFIRE SILENCE

Can we exchange brain waves in total silence?

A silence so loud I feel the throbbing of your pulse take me back in time when love was symbolic.

Trace hieroglyphics that cover your skin enough to resurrect sacred writings from within and illustrate them all over your...

I want to indulge in intellectual interactions, the kind that wets my paper.

The kind that allows me to tongue your brain down enough to remove all the IQ cumming from you.

Let us indulge in banter that discovers your ancient soul and unravels the roots of which you grow from.

Can I guide my hands across your body almost as if I were sculpting the female version of "the thinker?" Let me paint canvasses of faith within you.

I am not asking to touch you, but I just want to feel you.

Feel you so good I can restore you.

Heal you like medicinal remedies from the 18th century, can you hear me?

Exchange a silence so loud it fucks you into euphoria.

We share an addictive conversation that gently undoes all the pain within us.

I imagine as we kiss slowly, like hourglass sand, you fall for me.

Your eyes, they speak to me with the words of God.

Can I hug you like the reflection of the ocean and silently bang my currents into you as we both release orgasmic cries?

Let's exchange a silent emotion too tender for words to express, it mystifies your heart.

Carve trust along the walls of your flesh & create a resting tomb for a silent hieroglyph against the temple of your womb and be born again so we can stop being two.

Can we be deeper than lovers and fools?

Breathe a silence so loud it intoxicates our innocence.

Let's be both student and teacher.

Research each other to decipher the love we mummified for so long and unveil our primitive natures that revert us back to where it all began.

There is an art of symbolism that lies within the silence of our love.

Can we exchange brain waves so loudly I silently walk in your thoughts like I am on a pilgrimage in search of spiritual significance?

Let's exchange heart beats in a silent hieroglyph.

St. Petersburg

HAVOC

She was the kind of woman who was beautifully complicated.

In her simplicity lied a natural disaster waiting to break free, free from harsh realities she barricaded herself in.

The act was animated to say the least.

I was convinced at one point the old her was inexistent and outdated.

She trained herself to be actively immune to the very truth of who she was at her core.

There existed a mirror reflection she avoided.

She had a smile that could heal the pain of open wounds, but was so in tune with her personal baggage, and prepared to shatter you too.

The kind of woman to weep over your loss with no tears, then one day come and leave roses on your love tomb.

They say life is kind of funny.

The same things that keep you alive might even kill you.

I am thinking she must have been tired of wearing it all, well so was I.

She found comfort in being alone, well so did I.

However, in this game of baring it all, I can't keep being strong when you act like you don't care at all.

Look at the situation!

The unknown got me intimidated, so I illustrate it.

I pick up the phone to call and instead I'm reaching in my back pocket to write another love rhyme, another hate line, another misplaced lie, another thought kept to myself, but I guess maybe next time.

History must be repeating itself and if it isn't then there must be an ironic upside to this bona fide well-orchestrated homicide.

Tormented in despair, I was cast aside when she shut down.

Why was I not notified?

I wish I could take the confusion away.

I wish I could make you want to stay, but even in our final hours, my love for you will never go astray.

THUNDER STRANGERS

Like thunder in the late night, my heart roars for you.

Like the taste of morning dew kissing fields of grass, my tongue craves you.

I see what you are doing.

A mystery that goes hand and hand with sincerity, you control me.

I need rehab, I need intervention.

Nothing can help me.

My mind manipulates me.

You're no stranger to this.

You're no stranger to love, lust, and then repeat.

—For that night on the bench with CEV, where lost poets leave their work for a stranger to read.
Tampa, Florida 2016

EL VALOR DE UNA MUJER BILINGÜE
(THE VALUE OF A BILINGUAL WOMAN)

The value of a woman who resonates the streets with a voice that speaks the history of plena, of bomba, of mambo, o de salsa; When she speaks of sancocho, pernil, y de arroz con habichuela, it is priceless.

Y si no te gusta, no se que te pasa.

You see there is nothing sexier than the native Spanish tongue.

That same bilingual hypnotizing got you sprung kind of woman you will find in the kitchen tocando the latest of El Gran Combo, Willie Colon, y Hector Lavoe.

Salsa on 2's, that Latin hustle.

I hear the Spanish language and I am melting like piraguas on a hot sunny day.

Speak to me in your Spanish dialect, from Castellano to Puerto Rico I am addicted to your bilingual.

Like the best kind of perico, freshly served in the morning for breakfast.

"Ven a comer"!

You sound so sexy it should be illegal.

As you greet me con una tasa de Bustelo y un plato de avena.

O mejor un pedazo de Pan sobao, she speaks to me.

La negra tiene tumbao, is she related to Celia because I swear it on the sign of the Cruz she is my diabetic rush, dulce como azùca!

She is the essence of rhythm and blues.

The sazon in the words of my grace and el adobo knows it's place.

The cuchi frito to my late-night cravings.

She is Gran Canaria.

El miel sobre mi frangollo.

Y pero mija, tienes un poco de criollo that hums from between your lips you make it difficult to resist.

She is the likes of the 16th century ancestry bloodline, desde España hasta aqui.

El valor de una mujer bilingüe es all this world needs.

—For all Latin Women who embody the roots of their origin.

Chapter 3

FAMILY TREE

INSIGHT

Addressing your roots is super critical in your journey of healing and growing. We must never forget where we come from, but also understand that where we come from makes us or breaks us. *Family Tree* provides the reader a look into some particularly important people in my life. While some of these words may strike some chords, this is raw, real, and true. I struggled tremendously with this chapter because as a writer and poet, you want to produce the best and most perfect product. Illustrating who each of these individuals are required a deeper look at my life to the core. In writing these poems I learned that I love my family regardless of who they are, no matter their past, present, and DNA. I understand we are all different but cut from the same cloth. They serve a greater purpose for me. Without any of them, I would unequivocally be lost.

Parental Advisory

A young love filled with all of what the 80's lifestyle had to offer.

There was music for the disco, music for the perico, and music for the soul.

Santeria services, salsa y plena, and mornings filled with a hot cup of joe.

Two Afro-Latinos in love lust over what was never meant to be, but God had different plans for their eternity.

His dress shirt open just enough to reveal his masculinity and bell bottoms that accentuated her curves enough to entice his urges.

This was the beginning years of my parents.

They were two dynamic lovers who during their time of butterflies created me amid their wild nights up on East 86th St. at El Corso's, Home of Latin Music.

The years go on as they grew apart.

My parents became the sun and moon lost in the abyss of the stars on those tainted high nights.

They loved their kids and hated each other or that is how they made it seem.

Ironic, when addiction was present so was their peace and companionship.

Some day's dialogue with my parents consisted of reminders that even in grudge and denial we can still express 'I Love You' with things like, "Tell your mother I love her" and

"Tell your father he owes me money, that mother fuck'a".

During my childhood years his absence caused more damage than the scars embedded in my memory.

During my childhood years, her absence taught me to be a fortress of strength, not a punching bag for the weak.

As an adult, mom became my only constant.

Yet, even in her consistency, she certainly fell short as a mother, especially when it was time to party.

I guess my parents weren't so 'day and night' after all.

I guess they were still learning.

I guess my brother and I were worth all their fights.

I guess as adults him, and I can understand your story and the troubles you had.

I guess…is equivalent to almost and we all know "almost doesn't count".

What does count is how in their own ways they always made it known we were loved.

We traveled, made memories, broke bread together and shared holidays together.

They taught us to remain the red string that kept us attached to our roots, near and far.

Despite the overcast of dark shadows in their closet full of skeletons, these bins sitting in my closet full of memories captured in photos, illustrates a different idea of who they were.

I read messages on the back side of photos in my father's writing reminding my mother of what they share and how much he loved her.

I saw photos where I memorized my mother's beautiful smile in my father's embrace, standing beside him proudly.

In the end, when my father's absence became permanent, I felt a guilt that lingered within his casket.

In the end I felt her regret and sadness.

In the end, the truth is their story will always live on because they created two children, making their roots everlasting.

In the end, there still existed **LOVE**.

JUNIOR

Time is irrelevant when we speak.

It's as though I traveled back to that last night, he & I spoke.

Oh brother, my brother, you sound familiar to me.

DNA is scary, yet interesting.

You sound like him, our father.

Regurgitating the same self-pitied stories with weak attempts to make yourself cry.

Two lost souls getting high together.

'Frick and frack'...

Crutches for self-created injuries and yet, I love you so.

I wonder how quick your sand is as I stand by and watch you struggle.

Oh brother, how I wish I had the strength to save you from your own misfortunes followed by unexplainable fortunes.

Please don't guilt me for your hamster wheel behaviors.

I cannot be the yes to your favors.

Oh brother, it pains me to see you slowly crumble.

Talent is wasted when I know you have what it takes to be an inspirational symbol.

I have no knowledge of the craftsmanship it may take to reconstruct a foundation you have destroyed since your youth.

Thus, I guide you with no map, no G.P.S.

Just words filled with no wisdom, but experience: Experience and truth.

Prideful of the name you carry, but where is the pride Junior?

Existing in a potential you tainted in the innocent eyes of your offspring.

I pray for your safety.

I pray for your success.

I pray for you daily because I believe God created you different from the rest.

I pray for your healing and understanding that despite where life may take us, we will always be equal.

—Ruben

MIRROR IMAGE BOYS

Sometimes in life you need a curve ball to really awaken your soul.

Sometimes you need something to remind you there is a greater purpose.

Then they were born, God's given gift to us all.

Twin to your father's features, identical to your mother's persona.

The change in their life was fast paced.

Growing up had to happen overnight.

Sometimes there is a recharge.

There is a small remake of all that makes mommy and daddy whole for a second time.

Then, the second born comes along.

Twin to your mother's features, identical to your father's persona.

I wonder how often you look at yourself in the mirror and see someone else.

How often we look at you and see someone great.

Two growing boys, like seeds planted in the Garden of Eden, creating man by the standard of God.

Your innocence rapidly dissipating as the hair on your face starts to grow in.

Your voices are changing and if I didn't know any better, we can't call you babies anymore.

A wit that can't be found in adults, but two hearts, as full and golden as the two people who made you can be discovered as the years go on.

My nephews, what did we do so right to deserve the gift of your life?

You were the message we all needed to unite.

—Josiah & Giovani

September 13th

When I held you for the first time, I couldn't fathom the idea of never holding you again.

You quickly became the melody of my heartbeat.

You were the harmony in the late-night symphonies that would chime within the walls of our home as I would watch you breathing and smiling in your sleep.

My dearest sunflower; how sweet are your dreams?

I would lean over to caress your cheek and kiss you tenderly.

I smothered you in a bassinet not big enough to fit all my love in there with you.

Every morning with you nestled in my arms was perfection.

Delighted by your baby scent, I was engulfed in a world where only you existed, only you mattered.

Your first tears made me cry as I would soothe your aching screams with humming and praying.

You would look over to me with your huge eyes not quite able to decipher what you were seeing, but my voice, my voice was a familiar comfort.

When I first held you, I couldn't picture life without you.

From diaper changes to your messy face while you learned to eat...

From nap time to bath time…every day with you was my favorite time.

Ironic, you are so much like me.

Sour patch kids won't ever be the same.

Your first birthday saddened me greatly, for I knew time was not my friend.

You were growing quicker than I had imagined.

You ran before you walked.

Your first words weren't the best, but who cares because laughter fills the room whenever you talked.

Your gibberish makes sense.

Your dancing is A-1.

You're truly a blessing and I will forever be grateful for you.

My Virgo princess, you are heaven sent.

—Jaelani

THE SAGA

My greatest distraction came to me in the form of 'life' where my prayers, my dreams, and science made all the stars align to create a masterpiece of God.

This was my solo journey through motherhood.

The news of your existence was a beautiful surprise.

It was nine months of growing pains, changes, and a roller coaster of emotions.

With my insides expanding, I could feel the sensations of butterflies tickling the walls that protected you.

Your movements excited me and hurt at the same time.

You would leave me smiling after every kick and every flip, especially at night.

274 days of my roots nurturing you to perfection.

No one ever said this would be easy, but the power of a woman's body goes without saying.

I fully intend on raising you just as strong.

The might in your hands, the swiftness in your feet, the gentleness in your eyes, and those chubby cheeks; I wonder what else of you will be.

While you sleep, I pray the moon touches your soul.

When you rise, I pray your days are as bright as the sun and filled with joy.

And all that is in between may it always be a reminder you will always have me.

You have continuously been part of my story.

Unknown to me, but this leap of faith has been my greatest glory.

I thank my guiding angels for helping you choose me to be your mommy.

—Amaia

Blended

When people ask me about my family, I will share with them how perfectly blended we are.

I will tell them when I found love in you, I found a greater love in them.

And though they were not my own children, they certainly were my children.

When I signed up to be the bonus mom, I had no idea how full my heart would be with a son and daughter.

I walked into this life clueless, but if this was part of God's master plan, then its been an honor.

My days have been brighter because of my favorite pre-teens.

Always full of surprises and testing my limits.

Some days we were like milk and oil, unable to mix, and other days we were the perfect dose of blended chaos.

A chaos so calming it only made sense to us.

We were the dream team.

Family game nights were full of laughter and competition and movies nights were more like conversation nights because we all always had something to say.

They were the best combination of Ying and yang.

The absence of their bickering was strange to me.

After all, what siblings get along all the time without putting up a fight to get their own way?.

Playing the bad guy was no easy feat.

Being the good guy wasn't either, but nighttime was a favorite for me.

Coming home to them sound asleep.

My days were never complete without kissing them goodnight and wishing them sweet dreams.

Life without them is unfathomable.

The two so different in every way, but how they loved me each day without boundary was special to me.

Some words I find difficult to say because the truth is, I may not always be perfect in their eyes, but their innocence can never be tainted in my mind.

I may disappoint them sometimes, I may say a white lie too, but if I am giving my truth, family is what you make of it and being part of their life was all my puzzle needed to be completed.

—Lyric & Eros

Chapter 4

FUNERAL – DADDY'S DEMISE

INSIGHT

Death changes a person no matter how well you believe you can handle it. This is a self-explanatory set of poems dedicated to my father. This chapter targets my grieving process. My father's demise is still a difficult part of my life to accept, however, I found courage to just write. Him and I did not speak often, but when we did, I experienced joy and disappointment all at once. Now that I can't talk to him, I revisit these poems to remind myself of the beauty he helped me create. With that being said, I am grateful for the light he shined on my path of life. Though his absence pains me tremendously, his spirit continues to guide me. I hope in times of death, my readers can find an outlet and allow themselves the chance to create something passionate and beautiful. Remember, leave nothing unsaid.

Run, Fly, Butterfly

On my run today I felt the wind beneath my feet almost as if you were guiding me.

I looked into the distance, and I was met by a butterfly.

I guess death has a funny way of keeping someone alive.

They say when you see one it's a sign. So, I start talking to myself like I have traveled to a place in time where I could hear you, I could feel you, and I can breathe you.

Some days seem longer than others, most days I seem stronger than the others, but every day I find ways to fill a void I never expected would exist.

On my run today I felt the wind singing beneath my steps.

The echoes of your family crying, I wasn't sure if it was pain or regret because at times we laughed and others we sat in silence reminiscing about your artful ways.

Speak about your giving days. Your robbing slays. Then something eerie would take place like the lights would flicker.

This room once filled with sadness and numbing sensations was overcome with the belief that you were present warming the place with echoes of your laughter and love.

On my run today I could see your silhouette in the shadows that followed me.

My mirror image, I guess death has a funny way of teaching you about yourself because I was more like you than I had suspected.

All these years came and went our bond had been neglected. Made me wonder, if I had checked in one more time, called one more time…

Would it have been any different? Or was your demise this soon destined to take place because where I'm at these days, how I feel this way, some things I can't bring myself to say.

I mean it has no place. I got to let GOD have a talk with the beast in me.

Need help to find strength to overpower this denial of your final hour.

I grieve! Not many know my brain is a mess. Try to piece it all together, need to keep it all together.

Got to be strong for the rest. Guess I'm not allowed to be weak for a minute, just breathe for a minute.

Exit the room for a minute, as they closed your casket.

The whole ride to your resting place, I couldn't seem to look passed it.

I couldn't seem to outlast this messed up, cold, emptiness that lingered in that room.

I kicked! I punched! I walked, carrying you in disbelief.

Confusion painted my face, my gut filled with guilt, I cried!

Dear God, speak to me of forgiveness.

STAGE 1

I wish somebody would have told me that this pain was a constant.

That your absence was a concept my heart couldn't comprehend, and my mind wouldn't grasp it.

I wish I were given warning signs like, "use caution", but instead I was given things like limited time and vivid memories of your self-destruction.

Life didn't come equipped with a manual, but if it did, I'm sure the bond would have been automatic.

It's crazy how DNA keeps us connected like those phone calls we made and never connected.

Empty promises and full excuses left my innocence in a space trapped in traumatic.

Every time you seen me, then hugged me, I swear that shit was like magic because you would weep like a broken little boy and leave stains of your tears on shoulders heavy enough to still feel light, but cold enough to still feel numb...I stared at you lifeless.

In hindsight I believe you felt there was a slight resentment, even if there was, I loved you plenty.

I tried finding ways to drown out the pain but my tolerance for this henny isn't the same and my tolerance for acceptance wasn't either, because you would give me every last penny in your pocket if I let you, hoping it would make up for lost time when really I never needed that.

I know your love was never ending.

I still have that voice mail in my files. I guess it's taking much longer to digest this loss.

I can't help this phase of denial. Playing back that 10 second clip keeps from being suicidal. I've gone months pretending but the more I bleed here the more I realize these confrontations I have with my emotions have become my rival.

There isn't anything anyone can say when mourning has begun, I just ran from its arrival.

These days distraction seems to be my only means of survival.

1,000 WORDS LESS

I've rehearsed numerous ways to tell you how my grief is far greater than your absence and how your absence is far greater than any pain I have ever imagined.

If I attempted to connect this pain with paper, you would see letters dripping with regret like tears falling from my cheeks wetting an empty chest where her father's hands once rested.

A room filled with a warmth so cold you can see the chill of my breath as I sobbed over your body, and I never rehearsed it.

The grapevine says "A picture is worth 1,000 words" so in that moment, I loved you in 1,000 ways I couldn't put into words.

I loved you in 1,000 ways and still couldn't shake the hurt.

Every tear felt the same, draining.

I'm not sure what part of all this is worse you're missing in action in life or you're missing in action in death, but I pray you found comfort in that blue hearse.

I pray you found peace where we lied you to rest, and I pray you can feel this energy every time you inspire a new verse.

I'd give anything to have a second in your embrace where I could smell the residue of your Joop cologne and cigarette smoke embedded in your hard-working skin. Hair combed back, jeans and boots drenched in paint, a smile on your face, and sin in your pocket.

Deadly enough, rehab couldn't save you.

I'd give anything…anything, to not have to bury you this way.

JUNETEENTH HIS WAY

The Emancipation Proclamation was announced by Abraham Lincoln on September 22, 1862.

September 22, 1965, you were born.

Your first born made her debut September 20, 1988.

Three years prior was the first time you experienced your first high.

Ironic as it seemed because you gave me life, but as intoxicating as my love for you was, this daddy-daughter relationship wasn't enough of an addiction to keep you alive.

You were imprisoned by the likes of cocaine, marijuana, and cheap beers.

Guilt was freedom to the realities of what I now must dream of.

Your weeping and boy who cried wolf stories were a portmanteau of my daily celebrations of your life, except there were no joys dancing through my feet and no traditional songs humming from my lips like; "swing low sweet chariot"

History! June 19th, 1865, formerly enslaved people in Galveston rejoiced in the streets, but June 19th, 2018, in the slums of Puerto Rico, Newark & Perth Amboy New Jersey, people gathered in your name sharing lines of white powdery substances and ice cold Medallas.

However, I mourned you just as I did when you were alive. I sat at a bar in keeping with a tradition you began, alone, just as I felt when you were alive.

Vague memories resurfaced every so often at the age of 30.

I reminisced of my 26th…27th birthday when you looked into my distraught honey suckled eyes, as you foamed from your mouth and reeked of regret. This is how I found out. You uttered, "Happy birthday pumpkin, daddy loves you".

Eyes blood shot, hands swollen and rough. This image of you on repeat, how could I not memorize every let down you left me with?

Beaten into your demise.

Traditionally, Juneteenth marked the end of slavery. Your addiction marked the beginning and end for me. Where I was torn like the flesh of my ancestors as the begged for mercy. Torn between freedom and emancipation. Your death was total separation from me, but total freedom for you.

You made history dad. You went out the only way you knew how to go in.

Juneteenth, proclaimed as a holiday where heritage, culture, and freedom were observed through songs and cookouts. Juneteenth of 2018 was no holiday for me as I envisioned you sniffing your last lifeline proclaiming you no longer had any fight in you.

June 19th, 2018, you were freed of pain, of addiction; you were freed! You were freed! Rest in peace, on Juneteenth.

DEMISE

Your death dismantled me into fragmented portions of who you were.

I sat in silence for hours at a time starring at your still body, clothed in a brand-new suit and anchored by your blue tie, silk just like your hair. I sat in disbelief waiting for the slightest of movement in your hands.

I am haunted by the scent of all the flowers in that room.

Flowers you could not smell.

Flowers you should have had when you were alive.

Flowers for the dead because the reality was, life was too rough for you to survive.

The slamming of your casket, the clatter of the funeral door exit, the slamming...

The slamming still echoes in my head.

Traumatized by my greatest fear, death.

The hymns of my screams when I watched your brothers carry you out of the cold room that housed your body for over 24 hours, could awaken the souls I have lost prior to you.

Time just stood still.

All that was in motion was the realism of your forever absence and the sounds of my weeping as my tears slammed into the concrete.

I wonder now, if, right outside the doors of the funeral home where that cracked, untamed driveway exists, there grew a rose from my pain.

My pain so easily caught and dragged away from your hearse, as the muscle of my uncles pulled me away from what was possibly the very last time I could ever embrace you.

Cinder block walls surrounding me as I pounded my fist into them, exerting every bit of my anger.

That damn car ride to the cemetery.

The music that followed our steps as we led your body to its resting place where you and your father meet again.

How ironic it seems to be that your casket was as heavy as the emptiness within me.

Your death dismantled every strong fiber of my being.

Your demise was the beginning of my regret and healing all in one.

Chapter 5

FOREVER

INSIGHT

Forever, is however long you make it, even with breaks in between. One of the greatest things in life is to love and be loved. Everyone is in search of it, and I genuinely believe there is someone for everyone. In this chapter I share with you the honeymoon phase, the changes, the regrets, the temporary and the forever. All of which surround the subject of me and my greatest love of life. I have never felt this kind of love. It has been my purest, my sweetest, most romantic, and challenging relationship I have ever had. While the times have changed, I know much like many people who live in regret, wish they had a second chance. When life hands you a journal and quill pen, make poetry with the love of your life and let no pages bring you apart. Take no opportunity for granted.

FOREIGN SYMPHONY

She's always been a silent lover until our bodies came together like the perfect set of sheet music creating tunes that could crack a bass speaker in two.

I'd gently turn her dial and raise the volume in her enough to make her sacred walls collapse into pieces of what now is my favorite concerto.

I would study the tips of my fingers as they would strum along the vibrations of her best kept secret.

Causing intense out cries that could only be heard in the abyss of her maternal temple, as she would sing to me in an acapella that could make any conductor stall.

Her hands would meet my back carving lyrical remedies dating back to the climactic love we shared in a past life, overseeing ourselves on stage like an opera, rated R, but sophisticatedly proper.

I enjoyed role playing so much, I couldn't resist her gentle caress against my gold platted harp.

My heart orgasmed for her.

Together we were like oxygen distribution to my body.

Just sharing space with her made me want to fuck her into poetry and swallow her like the last bit of red wine dripping from the tip of my saxophone.

Her moans were inhaled and released like a perfect love jones.

She was the alchemy I've craved so desperately, the tender touch to my growing pains.

Oh love, a tender trap.

You send blood flowing through my veins straight to the devil's doorbell.

Twin flames igniting thunder & lightening together we are hot flashes of harmony.

Crashing satisfactions booming louder than a treble and as gentle as a violin.

Let us come together like a cymbal crash.

Oh, sweet symphony though I speak of you as if Mozart created you intentionally, you are foreign to me.

She was foreign to me.

DEAR THERAPIST

I don't feel like I use to, and I know it's easier to blame someone else but really, she makes me want to write her name all over my notebook like I'm trapped in an old school recess dream.

She intoxicates by touch, entices me when she speaks.

She leaves me jaded like five-star meals seasoned with a dash of curiosity.

A soothing fountain of youth, I am forever young.

It's an art this generation has lost sight of.

I was blinded, but we read each other like braille.

Refreshing like sweet morning dew, full of light, and kissed by the sun.

She is my shooting star when I am trapped in a corn maze, guiding me like the shine of a full moon when I am lost,

Oh, and then there is music.

She's like the shower song I sing from the depths of my soul with no auto tune, but she hypes me up anyway.

It's a love language we speak so well.

She finishes my sentences like, "knees weak, arms are heavy…" My rappers delight.

Dear therapist,

I don't feel like I use to, and I know it sounds a bit farfetched because it hasn't been much time, but she awakens my deeply rooted demons.

She's the king and queen pinnacle of cups, the tarot to my deck, the meditation pulsating from within my blood vessels.

I know myself.

Dear therapist,

I will be a fool for her time and time again even if we remain just friends because she's taught me how a smile is worth happiness with no end.

Anxiety is lost.

I am on a constant …high…energy vibrations echoing within these gas chamber walls.

I want to suffocate in her aura.

Be forever haunted in my evening hours of her innocent torments, her bountiful consents, and be engulfed in the reminder to live in the moment, but not with regret.

Dear therapist,

This has become addictive. I find myself sitting beside waters that connect us.

Mastering Yemaya's enchanted purpose.

Studying the blueprints that mural her silk skin, she is walking art.

My mind, a scandalous perversion of the words we follow and praise every Sunday.

She is doses of marijuana.

She is cases of Heineken and Gem pizza, with Frank Sinatra playing in the background.

Optimistic, on free weekends, we indulge in green apple Moscato for we are simply wine glasses, sweet and half empty, but together all full.

Dear therapist,

You can have your mirror back because when she looks at me, I don't feel like I use to.

DINNER DATE

We are late for everything.

We're caught up in conversation, losing track of time.

Our flukes filled just enough to drown in a curious nervousness.

I watch the rise and fall of every fizz after each sip, like my blood pressure as it fills my body with heat.

You make me bubble, I burst from within.

Your eyes they tell a story.

I am focused on you, your beau.

Your hair, it sits against your skin at just the right angle, enough to hide the blush that paints your face.

My palms are sweaty. Your cheeks are full.

You smile and my heart begins racing.

Your words pause mid-sentence to catch mine as they sail off my tongue only to meet mid-air.

Together we drip in lust.

Together we melt in temptation.

Together, we dine like no one is watching.

Together in silence, we are in love, but together we are patient.

You ordered your meal.

I ordered mine.

Let's toast to us and a great night.

We sat by the mountains and the waiter set the mood.

Our body language was intense.

Our appetite was impressed.

In my mind I devoured you a million times.

Told the waiter, no thanks to dessert, my date will do just fine.

ROSES AND THORNS

The space between us feels so cold.

Isn't it ironic considering we are the perfect temperature for a room full of roses that only exist in memory?

I can feel us fighting the urges to physically connect.

I am torn with my sentiments.

Every time you walk past me, I can feel myself sadden even more, wondering if you are living in regret.

I crave -you- are equivalent to drugs never consumed, yet so familiar to me

You sedate my vulnerabilities; I cannot resist you.

We sit with just inches between us, and it feels so awkward.

Heavy breathing echoing within the walls of our home but feels more like a house.

The slamming of our thoughts piercing through the clacking of dishes.

I've been waking up to an empty bed full of thorns aching within the foul words we shared over dead roses in dire need of watering and nurturing

3a.m. everyone is sound asleep.

The silent never felt so loud.

Alone even with your company.

My tears are running dry waiting for answers that we both haven't found.

This is borderline insanity, but I see clearly now.

Everyone is born with their own roses and thorns.

Maybe, just maybe, without the thorns our roses cannot exist.

Just maybe we are grooming each other to be the gardener we manifested in our dreams.

HOPE

We were two misguided lovers walking amongst the contradictions of the 1500s infamous proverbs, *forgive and forget*.

It felt all too familiar.

She became the scratched vinyl playing in the background of her stories filled with holes and confusion.

Stories that confirmed her heart had been abused and played with.

Even knowing the challenges, I would be facing, I tried flying with a dragonfly that did not have a place for this blue butterfly.

Swarming over meadows of sunflowers and lilies, they were all created so differently, yet sounded the same, like rustling old paper filled with biblical scriptures we tried so desperately to live by every Sunday, yet that dissipated like the melting of the body of Christ.

We planted seeds of a life together.

Even drowned out the pain with after hour melodies strumming over the words that haven't stopped echoing since you tainted my ears with static.

A static so loud.

It was like oceans in seashells that washed away like the last bit of the salt residue staining my face with tears awaiting to resume flowing like the Mekong River.

We used Tibetan meditations to find healing, yet on my solo journey, I continued to gravitate to the broken.

I made myself believe I could repair a silhouette even her shadow wished to forget.

Yet, here we were, trying to perfect the art of gardening as we nurtured each other's roots with tenderness, love notes that whispered sweet everything's, and random wrap your arms around my waist kiss me moments to remind us of that special kind of feeling that could only exist between the good, bad, and the ugly bits of us.

There we were hanging pretty, painted pictures of our galactic love and music playing in an octave that only sent vibrations through half of what was once us.

I am left with scrapped knees praying with a void incapable of being filled with anything remotely close to how good she occupies my heart.

I been *HOPE*ing things change, and she return to me.

Love, if it isn't shared with you, it holds no meaning.

I am here for all eternity.

WE CANNOT BE FRIENDS

The concept just does not sit well with me after learning what life is with you at my side.

You cannot possibly believe I can unlearn loving you after everything we have been through.

Yet, I am here for the ride.

After all, setting you free may make me realize between us has always been the need to compromise & respect each other's life choices.

While this decision is not mine, I am keeping hope alive.

Perhaps during this time, we can experience the rebirth of the bee and honey like it once was.

In love, basking in the light of the sun as it guides us through a fairytale come true.

Perhaps the red string of fate can pull us back in like drugs do when we are going through withdraw.

You know I have had my fair share of mediocre women, however with you there was nothing but a rareness kind of feeling that occurred.

You once told me, "They don't make my kind in bulk", still I cannot help but walk up and down the aisles of places you have shared with me; all embedded in my memory attempting to replace the irreplaceable.

And not just any places either.

I am talking about the places only your kind of ecstasy can manifest.

I roam throughout life with a map hoping X marks the spot of where your heart still lies waiting for us to mend everything that made sense once upon a time.

A friendship, however, does not feel right.

You were exactly where my head would lay at night when my thoughts could not connect, and my brain just kept the fight.

You were exactly where my tears would fall when I felt the emptiness only you understood from the inside.

You were, you still are, more than enough and now I am not quite sure if breathing without you is how I envisioned us sharing in motherhood.

I mean, is there truly an expectation I will not want to hold you closely or kiss you gently?

Or not want to relive endless nights where we physically connected. Making passion sweat from wall to wall, I yearn for you.

Your tight embrace, squeezing my hand three times, cutting my circulation off, but making me smile.

Can you live without those sensations' day to day?

It is so silly at times how even when you are away, I manage to pull together another poetic line.

I cannot help but laugh because this pain of your absence, of your distance is much greater when I cry.

If I could sum up the courage to let go maybe you will find me in another life.

I cannot just be your friend.

How can we be so reluctant? I just want the same person I fell in love with.

Every time I see you, speak of you, think of you; every time, I cannot help but still see my future wife in you.

For C.A.H.M

Chapter 6

FRUITS OF THE HEART

INSIGHT

Fruits of the Heart tackles matters of the heart; the obvious. This chapter was inspired entirely after weeks of bible study and a continuation of the poetry in chapter 5. It has allowed me to truly reflect on what I have recently felt. Every piece stems from the seeds planted by 'Miel y Mango' (honey and mango). My best friend says, "when life hands you lemons, you make a margherita", but I believe lemons are bitter and that is why everything taste better with a drizzle of 'honey'. This chapter highlights the faith I have in reigniting a flame that was put out prematurely.

—For a Love Turned Blue

EMPTY PAGES

I tried to please every bit of you

I even tried being glue for those pieces of you that would not seem to keep together

I was a band aid for your pains and traumas

In return, I was left in the same condition I found you in.

There was a platform present for every occasion of hurt and disappointment.

Then there was silence and pages filled with a falsehood of what our love defined.

We latched onto each other like combination locks left on fences overlooking the poisoned waters off the coast of Jersey City's Bay area.

We jumped the broom without the ceremony, because like anything new, our honeymoon was just that, sweet as honey and far from our reach like the moon.

We lived in a world where only poets existed; writing each other off as if from beginning to end we were hamsters in our cycle of ups and downs.

We lived in a world where no matter the struggle, we were set in our commitment but somehow we broke.

Every low destroyed our foundation. Every high confused us.

It was a rollercoaster of soap opera scenes filling our days like she was addicted to her leading role and I her co-star who self-imploded waiting to kill off my character.

I asked for consistency often...

She asked for my calm after every storm...

We turned our backs on each other every night to make love to our journals and little black books of memories to only remind us of our happy times.

Our memories were few or one too many, but there came a point where things had to change because we threw our path away.

We should have never let pain push our love astray.

I tried to please every bit of you, but I failed.

Here I am, standing in that very spot I imagined us getting married in waiting for you to meet me somewhere in the middle of our table of contents, where you help me rewrite us with the same quill pen you began our story with.

Here I am empty, like the pages I tried so desperately to read within you attempting to make sense of why I left to begin with.

FROM SCRATCH

With time I grew spoiled with having you around.

Your absence was felt, but I have to remind myself to keep shooting.

We have always been strong enough to bare the recoil, if you disagree than why are you still my target?

She said we communicated so well, but when push came to shove, she wasn't so well.

That's why I buried my pen into some paper, let the man speak to the beast in me.

When things started going wrong, I came writing at his gates, like God bring peace in me.

I heard silent screaming coming from the misplaced, innocent girl trapped within her spirit.

Her angry tears crashing like David and Goliath in combat.

I sensed the love she lacked; I was just looking to provide that.

Having control fueled her ego.

With all that pride, her character was lethal.

It took sanity to fight insanity or maybe we both were just as crazy for one another.

I began coming to terms with her being my rock bottom.

She was just a caliber dose of reality at a time for me.

Her flaw like beauty came free of vanity.

Truth was, she was my alchemy, and the way poetry was constantly born, it's safe to say she was part of my anatomy.

They say the weak need the strong, so if you be my Troy, then I'll be your coward, except, unafraid to fight for you.

If you want to be hot and cold, I'll pay your water bill.

If the lights go out, we just need to restore its' power.

But, when war comes, be still.

WE can start from scratch and reinvent our final hours.

STAINED GLASS WINDOW

We gathered amongst strangers to share the word of GOD every Sunday.

In our best dress, seated to the left mostly.

Taking notice of the stained windows and their constant signs.

We sat where FAMILY was present often and the last time we existed together in church the HOLY SPIRIT sent his message.

MARRIAGE engraved in the small, but mighty window occupying the hallway of the restroom.

In that moment I could feel the smile of my soul come to life as I stood before the woman I prayed for.

God GRACE me with the PATIENCE to wait on your readiness to be my wife.

Guided in his light, I prayed we would eventually reunite.

I understood the meaning behind 'not by power nor by might' that we would live a fruitful life.

The scriptures spoke so prominently every visit we made.

There was HOPE in every line Pastor read and LOVE with every blessing he gave.

We gathered amongst strangers to PRAISE the Lord, except this time I sat without you just a few pews behind, wishing for some eye contact.

I left my tears in the shirt I wore that day grieving more than I had expected, but I believe the deliverance of all that was PEACE was provided to us in every way.

We even gathered at the stroke of midnight for Christmas one day.

Just me, you, and this ring.

Receiving the body of Christ wasn't just for the souls' nourishment, we were anew weekly, but daily we had a FAITH together strong enough to combat anything the devil sent our way.

I believe God knew my name when I heard him talk to me as I kneeled and prayed.

My weeping would bring your hand to gently be placed on my shoulder and sometimes you embraced my hand making sure I was okay.

Our days in CHURCH were shortly lived, but 'I Can Only Imagine' that you and I will return to where we first began to reconcile our differences.

PATIENCE

In my loneliness I continue checking my phone every time it chimes in the distance hoping it is you.

If I'm being any honest, I even changed your ring tone, so I know when your words come through.

The problem is I'm waiting for something that won't ever come true.

In the hours when I should rest, insomnia hits.

I feel slightly crazy as I reach for my phone to text you once again.

I wish I had a couple of forever's to use this time around, like a personal genie ready to grant me three wishes as if they all wouldn't be to bring you back so you would stay this time around.

Retrograde seems to get the best of me when Neptune's in my seventh house.

Patiently waiting for the orbit to realign with my greatest intensions.

I knew this was all a sacrifice.

I continue to grieve you in life and others in death.

In the time of butterflies, I wonder if I can accidentally on purpose connect with you, like shooting stars sailing in the night skies when hope seems afar; as the sun sets and the moon rises, my hearts bursting with joy, I wonder if this is the big bang you spoke of to your children when love was created, and memories were captured.

I remain haunted by the scent of your after shower.

I remain haunted by the mistakes the devil so easily influenced and here I am manipulating the power in my word play, trying to bridge the gap between us for God's sake.

Day dreaming has become addictive as I train my soul's ache to be conditioned without you.

And when he speaks to me all I hear are the voices of our guardian angels saying, "be patient".

Waiting is never the easiest thing to do, but I have found an infatuation in trusting in the word of the Lord.

In times of our vulnerability, we exchange conversations in the dark only to shed light on the truths of our missteps and obtain forgiveness without hoarding the sentiments of any regret and resentment.

For that is not what this journey requires.

When I stop to visit the waters of the Earth, I revert to the fruits of my spirit, asking for the deliverance of amendment because if there is no renovation to the foundation, then there cannot be contentment and if there be no contentment then we cannot exist in commitment.

Thus, I remain patient.

I keep moving forward, but I am relentless in this battle, because we all know love can be a war at times.

My efforts go uncontested because this type of ever after is an investment.

I know without the payment of patience, my faith is nothing more than an enchantment, and we are not living in a fairytale.

For you I will wait.

For you I will carry enough faith.

For you I remain.

The Suitcase

You came with baggage of all sorts and lucky for me I enjoyed traveling.

I took on the luxury of being on vacation every day.

Running through security checks and gates of the smallest and biggest airports.

When we would land I called it the free ports because I would help you unpack just enough to make the weight a little lighter and your smile a little brighter.

In short, I will always be your life support.

Some days the turbulence struck all too often.

My patience would run low, but my travels never brought me down from the clouds

it has been mighty exhausting.

I am not sure if I ever understood them, but if every world map were written on you, I would not mind being lost then.

I unravel the tiniest pieces of your baggage in these hidden compartments as we continue our travels and that is how it all started.

To my dear dearly departed, it has been a rough time, but I do not mind the frequent stops or the hours of darkness.

Traveling with you is inspiration at its hardest.

If my last stop be here, I thank you for making me an artist and to show you my appreciation baby you can have the window seat.

When you get stuck in the middle, I can help you find comfort by letting you rest your head on me so you can sleep to the rhythm of my heartbeat.

No matter the destination I want no one else beside me.

Before we get to our next stop let me store your suitcase up top, but if u chose to leave it behind we can call it free space and keep it moving.

It is hard to forget things so when the flight attendant says take notice of the emergency doors, I am thinking which one of us will be first to exit.

I strap in my seat belt and rearrange my thoughts like we are both trapped in a game of Tetris.

I find the deepest knots of loathing in my stomach, but it is not about me and my fear.

Suddenly you reach your hand out and I grab on.

We exchange looks as we ready for this journey with baggage or not, I'm not afraid if it hurts me.

And for hours we fly in silence.

Putting years into our mileage

Jet blue, American airlines, United.

Baggage claim can be done at carousel #7.

I am in no rush.

Just get us there safely.

I may help unload the carriage, but you get us to where we're going like a well-seasoned pilot

And I am alright being your co-pilot because the truth is your love is mighty to me.

Fill your baggage with happiness and grand memories and if I get weak if you get stuck there is no use in fighting.

We can replace and repair the engine for our next vacation.

SECOND CHANCES

Second chances come few, never many when guided by judgement and opinions that are unwelcome, unwanted, and never friendly.

There is an unspoken fight between two souls followed by the existence of rooms filled with envy where they coexist.

I broke my head putting together a puzzle that created the greatest of master pieces.

I took blow after blow like iron fists striking my gut.

I got up, I did it again and again.

You placed walls in my way, and I chipped away until you couldn't resist.

I needed to reach my friend, I needed to give you my best, I wanted the storm to rest thus, I prayed on every thought you roused.

I created moments that would last forever, and recorded happiness bonded in our mind like a broken record so I can revisit them in your absence.

Fear controlled every move I made.

Do it right the first time so we do not need second chances or the uncertainty of faith.

You became an addictive habit.

No rehab could help ease the fein in my sadness.

Every day was colder than the last, but something in me believed I wasn't left abandoned.

You came & went with keys incapable of duplicity, so if you returned, I'd let u back in

admittedly.

I faced us optimistically.

Felt your wrath every time you faced me judiciously, but to all creditability, we were nothing less than serendipity.

In your arms I wanted to spend an eternal epiphany of when I first found you, when I second met you.

Falling in love with you was déjà vu.

I was uplifted, this feeling was herbal.

You became the beginning and end of my journal where you remained encrypted in the depths of my solitude.

While protecting my closet of skeletons I am fighting to love you.

An internal inferno, where I am sleep deprived, but I love you most when I am nocturnal.

Together we defeated the elements of whatever odds we rummaged though.

pt2.

We grew up, I love you too.

—*For my inner person. For she shines in times of trouble but hides in times of grace, but loves hard.*

Chapter 7

FIN

INSIGHT

The last of *For Blue Butterflies* is completed by this final chapter. These very personal poems that have defined my darkest of days where I felt lost, empty, and alone. I overcame self-destruction with my poetry. The first step in overcoming depression and the first step towards healing must start with being self-aware. I am who I am today because I kept pushing through my trials and tribulations. It has taken me an exceedingly long time to get to this place. It has also taken a lot of tears, fear, disappointment, anger, laughter, and love to rebuild the bits of me I let others ruin. I am proud of the poet in me and the person I am.

CRY FOR HELP

The walls of my car know the sound of my tears as they crash into the fine fibers of the drivers' chair.

They know the havoc of my sadness and the darkness of my loneliness.

I blast the radio to drown out the broken tunes of the weeping soldier in me.

Only to check my rear view and realize that version of me is hurting too.

Switch the gears into drive, but I'm headed in no direction anytime soon.

Emotional damage has me paralyzed.

A smile presented as truth; do you see it too?

I'm self-imploding while encouraging others to speak out and start self-reporting as if every day for me lately hasn't been cold and stormy.

I let the eye of the hurricane tell my forecast daily.

I'm praying someone save me from this chaos.

Help me shed one less tear so I have the courage to wake up tomorrow for the aftermath I so desperately wish my brain would file under, suicide in exchange for life.

The walls of my car know the somber sounds of my weeping.

This crippling feeling of demons destroying a foundation I figured would be the perfect murder scene in a lifetime movie.

I wonder, would my story be worthy enough to exist on post cards that are mailed from one asylum to another millions of miles away.

I wonder if this type of insanity is acceptable these days because I hear voices often, they all tell me the same, not today.

I know myself far too well to be a stranger of pain, but if I could leave this all behind would you celebrate my name?

FREQUENCY

Sleep is the key to pausing the mind just enough to find a temporary peace.

Then REM stage begins, and my subconscious is awake just trying to keep the fight.

Like no one ever tells you there's no manual to the Game of Life you just live to survive for today's tomorrow and yesterday's goodbye.

Insomnia chokes me at a resting state, like a noosed rope bursting veins within my neck.

I've been enslaved to this guilt for feeling my feelings.

If I am still, then I prevail.

When I am still, I can exhale.

My breathing thrives through universal vibrations, I wonder if you feel me when we are distant.

Apologies become a habit, like how do I fix this?

Why does this always happen, but feel so different?

Steadily composing in silence because only then is when I win the war against being dismissed.

Sheltered in what you think is enough for me to release in.

Your cold tender way shows me plenty.

Past life regression has me wondering if I was you before we met.

Frequent patterns of disaster.

Demons chasing light, when will we get there, to a place of total freedom because I'm ready?

Slowly disrupting the dark shadows that occupy vacancies you allowed to become.

Dreaming awake until the next nightmare happens then I'm back to sleep wishing I never wake again.

This is all too familiar and all too frequent for my liking.

I just want to rest peacefully and stop fighting.

My Kindness for Weakness

I held you in such a high regard, but you took advantage of sleeves that carried my heart.

Your selfishness pushed me too far.

Your ignorance just keeps triggering things and each day comes and goes just as hard.

Spoken words are weakened by a silence so deadly and deafening, I bet in this moment I strike your raw nerve.

You respond with facial expressions that make you ugly and shrugs shivering with cold that make me hotter than the Earth's core.

I have been bearing far too much, maybe more than I even deserve.

Some plates others would not even step to let alone be a provider to her and yet 365 days I've been doing this full time, so for you to think any less of me as her mother is absurd.

I guess with some decisions come the truth that only caused us some hurt but if you were not ready for this type of responsibility then you should have protected yourself rather than lived through childbirth.

To say I never did anything for her was you showing your ungratefulness, it is no wonder you are a disappointment to those who must accept they created this.

I face a mirror daily looking for what is left of me because you almost destroyed me.

I came from a broken family, a product of child custody.

Thus, when I held my kid for the first time, I knew I would always be kept in good company.

Watching her grow is like a fairytale to me.

I am in disbelief God would even bless me this deep, so when I heard her utter the word mommy, I knew we were made for each other, and we connected spiritually.

I prayed for her endlessly then the stars aligned one night perfectly as the doctor placed you in my arms, I knew the true definition of heavenly.

I spent nights where I got no sleep.

I was too caught up in counting every chest rise as you breathed life into me.

For every tear shed and broken heart you may experience, for every inspiring moment and fear you may ever live in I need you to know the hover of my embrace was created to protect you and there was nothing in this world I would ever let defame you.

Nothing in this world would push me in a direction where it does not lead to you.

2:04 in the morning was the awakening of all that is glory.

I found a new reason to keep writing my story.

I remember when you started crawling, I cried because I knew time was not a friend of mine.

I remember when you started running, I cried because I thought where the rush was? you weren't even walking.

You are '1' now and you wake up talking.

Most days I must hear it on facetime or on snap chat because your mother and I can't have actual face time without snap backs.

At times I wish I could erase that and go back but if I regretted being in the same place as her that night then I wouldn't enjoy the pleasures of this life, right?

Every blood drop, sweat bead, tear, and fine fibers of my body is dedicated to shining a light so bright for my daughter that she would never know my resentment of you.

She will never know how much I bent over backwards and cried for you.

She will never know the levels of disappointment you bathed me in.

She will never know how many times you used her as a pawn to control me.

She will never know the many times you lied to make yourself look good, and I the bad guy.

She will never know the red flags you clothed me in.

She will never know the pain you caused me and how much power I gave you.

She will never know that even in our worse hours, you could not break me enough to stop me from watering my daughter's roots enough to watch her bloom and shine.

My little sunflower will never know anything less than love because no matter what mountains interfere with our journey, together my daughter and I could move them.

—You know who you are and I forgive you.

I WRITE

I write though I am uninspired by the uninvited guest who continues stealing my poetic mojo like we're playing cops and robbers.

I am hiding from the masses tracing my steps, past and present with heavy hated regret.

They are even trying to write my future for me, while I am trying to right my present.

The unwrapping and rewrapping of guilt, pain, and personal madness keeps taking place.

I write, rewrite, and then rap all that is life.

God's gift to me delivered in bright lights of white.

My guardian angels providing a path my feet are too afraid to follow.

My mind wanders through the chaos that exists in the soul of a poet.

Some failures were nearly capable of annihilating the strongest of my vessels.

So, I remain focused on every beat that strums my clarity and strength.

I can hear your desires for my thoughts.

These empty pages of journals are mourning the loss of who I once was.

I resurrect the sinner in me and release everything procrastination forced me to be.

I am no longer shackled by disappointment.

I write!

No longer prisoner of my own mind.

I write!

I'm no longer waiting on a muse to ignite a flame that has always burned ever so secretly.

I write everything that defines the true colors of who I am, Poetic Justice.

To my readers: Be unafraid to release everything that shackles your peace and love!

Poetic Justice

ABOUT THE AUTHOR

Born and raised in Perth Amboy, New Jersey, Jessica Irizarry came from a one parent home, but was raised by an entire village. She was a product of her own environment, where she experienced the highs and lows of traumas and the happiest of her days during her childhood. Writing began for her at the age of 12. At the age of 32, she now has an established career in law enforcement, two college degrees, and 18 years of experience in writing. Jessica has performed for numerous events ranging from raising awareness on domestic violence to AIDS awareness. She has been part of many open mic shows and on stage is where she delivers her best and most passionate work. Jessica is a graduate of New Jersey City University, where she found her courage and voice to be the poet and writer she is today. She has volunteered her time to be a peer mentor, a tutor for children from the ages 8 to 13, coached recreational soccer and softball teams, and has also volunteered her coaching expertise in a high school setting for a girls' basketball team. She prides herself in always providing her best self to those she may encounter in life. She is compassionate and passionate in all she does. Her being a poet is just one of many things that are amazing about her to say the least. Jessica is also part of The Book Publishing Academy, which was founded by Janine Hernandez. Through this opportunity, Jessica has become the best version of herself as a writer, however, the journey does not end here.

Connect with the author:

Instagram: Justicep0etry
Email: PoeticallyJess714@gmail.com

Jessica L. Irizarry
(Poetic Justice)
For Blue Butterflies

ENDORSEMENTS

"For Blue Butterflies is a poetry book full of life, and love. As an avid reader I feel alive through her words. A must read."

—Janine Hernandez, Author, Speaker, Book Coach

Janine Hernandez is an author, mentor, and speaker. She is the founder of the Book Publishing Academy. From as early as the age of 9, Janine knew she would become a world-famous self-published author, whose first-hand experiences would lend credibility to her work. True to her childhood dream, at the age of 26, Janine self-published her very first book. She coaches aspiring authors and speakers on how to self-publish their books. When Janine isn't reading or writing amazing stories, she loves to spend her time hiking, traveling, and exploring the world. She is an avid reader and is passionate about working on becoming the best version of herself from the inside out.

In 2011 Janine was awarded the Mitch Akin Mentor of the Year award for the New Pathways Program. Janine sits on the Board of Reach Family Services, a local nonprofit organization that focuses on assisting families, who are raising children with behavioral health and emotional challenges

Janine received her Master of Arts in International Business from Western International University and currently resides in Phoenix AZ. Janine is available for speaking events, keynote presentations, panel discussions, and life/motivational coaching.

The End